50 Farmers Market Meal Recipes for Home

By: Kelly Johnson

Table of Contents

- Caprese Salad with Heirloom Tomatoes and Fresh Mozzarella
- Grilled Vegetable Platter with Balsamic Glaze
- Ratatouille with Seasonal Vegetables
- Corn and Black Bean Salad with Avocado
- Zucchini Noodles with Pesto and Cherry Tomatoes
- Stuffed Bell Peppers with Quinoa and Kale
- Roasted Beet and Goat Cheese Salad with Walnuts
- Vegetable Stir-Fry with Tofu or Chicken
- Butternut Squash Soup with Apple and Sage
- Fresh Tomato Bruschetta with Basil
- Spinach and Feta Stuffed Mushrooms
- Grilled Eggplant with Tahini Sauce
- Summer Squash and Corn Chowder
- Kale and White Bean Soup
- Roasted Garlic and Tomato Pasta
- Cucumber Salad with Dill and Greek Yogurt Dressing
- Roasted Carrots with Honey and Thyme
- Panzanella Salad with Cucumber, Tomato, and Bread
- Sweet Potato and Black Bean Enchiladas
- Spinach and Mushroom Quiche
- Grilled Portobello Mushrooms with Balsamic Glaze
- Asparagus and Goat Cheese Tart
- Roasted Cauliflower with Lemon and Parmesan
- Fresh Pea Risotto with Mint
- Grilled Corn on the Cob with Herb Butter
- Rainbow Chard and White Bean Saute
- Tomato and Basil Galette
- Beet and Carrot Salad with Citrus Dressing
- Broccoli and Cheddar Stuffed Potatoes
- Green Bean Almondine
- Arugula and Strawberry Salad with Balsamic Vinaigrette
- Summer Vegetable Ratatouille
- Potato Leek Soup
- Stuffed Acorn Squash with Wild Rice and Cranberries
- Roasted Brussels Sprouts with Bacon and Maple Syrup

- Grilled Peaches with Honey and Yogurt
- Eggplant Parmesan
- Roasted Root Vegetable Medley
- Tomato and Basil Frittata
- Cabbage and Apple Slaw
- Grilled Halloumi with Watermelon and Mint
- Garlic Butter Roasted Mushrooms
- Kale Caesar Salad with Homemade Dressing
- Baked Parmesan Zucchini Fries
- Beetroot and Goat Cheese Tartlets
- Corn and Tomato Pie
- Butternut Squash and Sage Risotto
- Swiss Chard and Ricotta Stuffed Shells
- Grilled Vegetable Quesadillas
- Roasted Pumpkin Soup with Crispy Sage

Caprese Salad with Heirloom Tomatoes and Fresh Mozzarella

Ingredients:

- 2-3 large heirloom tomatoes, sliced
- 1-2 balls of fresh mozzarella cheese, sliced
- Fresh basil leaves
- Extra virgin olive oil
- Balsamic vinegar reduction (optional)
- Salt and pepper to taste

Instructions:

1. Arrange the sliced heirloom tomatoes and fresh mozzarella cheese on a serving platter, alternating them in a circular pattern or layering them.
2. Tuck fresh basil leaves between the tomato and mozzarella slices.
3. Drizzle extra virgin olive oil over the salad.
4. If desired, drizzle balsamic vinegar reduction over the salad for extra flavor.
5. Season with salt and pepper to taste.
6. Serve immediately as a refreshing appetizer or side dish.

Enjoy the vibrant colors and flavors of this classic Italian salad made with fresh, seasonal ingredients from the farmer's market!

Grilled Vegetable Platter with Balsamic Glaze

Ingredients:

- Assorted vegetables (such as bell peppers, zucchini, eggplant, mushrooms, cherry tomatoes, asparagus, and red onions)
- Olive oil
- Salt and pepper
- Balsamic glaze (store-bought or homemade)

Instructions:

1. Preheat your grill to medium-high heat.
2. Wash and prepare the vegetables. Cut the bell peppers, zucchini, and eggplant into slices. Leave the mushrooms whole or halve them if they're large. Trim the woody ends off the asparagus. Cut the cherry tomatoes in half. Cut the red onions into thick slices.
3. Place the prepared vegetables in a large mixing bowl. Drizzle with olive oil and toss to coat evenly. Season with salt and pepper to taste.
4. Arrange the vegetables on the preheated grill in a single layer. Grill for about 5-7 minutes per side, or until they are tender and have nice grill marks.
5. As the vegetables finish grilling, transfer them to a serving platter.
6. Drizzle the grilled vegetables with balsamic glaze just before serving.
7. Garnish with fresh herbs like basil or parsley, if desired.
8. Serve the grilled vegetable platter hot or at room temperature as a side dish or appetizer.

This dish is not only visually stunning but also bursting with flavor, making it a perfect addition to any meal or barbecue. Enjoy!

Ratatouille with Seasonal Vegetables

Ingredients:

- 1 large eggplant, diced
- 2 medium zucchinis, diced
- 1 large red bell pepper, diced
- 1 large yellow bell pepper, diced
- 1 onion, diced
- 3 cloves garlic, minced
- 4-5 ripe tomatoes, diced (or 1 can of diced tomatoes)
- 2 tablespoons tomato paste
- 2 tablespoons olive oil
- 1 teaspoon dried thyme
- 1 teaspoon dried oregano
- Salt and pepper to taste
- Fresh basil leaves for garnish

Instructions:

1. Heat the olive oil in a large skillet or Dutch oven over medium heat.
2. Add the diced onion to the skillet and cook until translucent, about 5 minutes.
3. Add the minced garlic and cook for another minute until fragrant.
4. Add the diced eggplant to the skillet and cook for about 5 minutes until slightly softened.
5. Next, add the diced zucchini, red bell pepper, and yellow bell pepper to the skillet. Cook for another 5 minutes, stirring occasionally.
6. Stir in the diced tomatoes, tomato paste, dried thyme, dried oregano, salt, and pepper. Allow the mixture to simmer for about 15-20 minutes, stirring occasionally, until the vegetables are tender and the flavors have melded together.
7. Taste and adjust the seasoning if needed.
8. Once the ratatouille is ready, remove it from the heat and let it cool slightly.
9. Serve the ratatouille warm, garnished with fresh basil leaves.

Enjoy this classic French dish featuring the best of seasonal vegetables from the farmer's market! It's perfect as a vegetarian main course or as a side dish to accompany grilled meats or crusty bread.

Corn and Black Bean Salad with Avocado

Ingredients:

- 2 cups cooked black beans (or 1 can, rinsed and drained)
- 2 cups cooked corn kernels (fresh, canned, or frozen)
- 1 ripe avocado, diced
- 1 red bell pepper, diced
- 1/2 red onion, finely chopped
- 1/4 cup chopped fresh cilantro (or parsley for a milder flavor)
- Juice of 1-2 limes
- 2 tablespoons extra virgin olive oil
- 1 teaspoon ground cumin
- Salt and pepper to taste

Instructions:

1. In a large mixing bowl, combine the black beans, corn kernels, diced avocado, diced red bell pepper, chopped red onion, and chopped cilantro.
2. In a small bowl, whisk together the lime juice, olive oil, ground cumin, salt, and pepper to make the dressing.
3. Pour the dressing over the salad ingredients in the large mixing bowl.
4. Gently toss everything together until well combined and evenly coated with the dressing.
5. Taste and adjust the seasoning if needed, adding more salt, pepper, or lime juice to taste.
6. Cover the salad and refrigerate for at least 30 minutes to allow the flavors to meld together.
7. Before serving, give the salad a final toss and garnish with additional cilantro leaves if desired.
8. Serve chilled as a refreshing side dish or light lunch.

This Corn and Black Bean Salad with Avocado is packed with fresh flavors, colors, and textures, making it a perfect dish to enjoy during warmer months or as a side at any gathering.

Zucchini Noodles with Pesto and Cherry Tomatoes

Ingredients:

- 4 medium zucchinis
- 1 cup cherry tomatoes, halved
- 1/2 cup basil pesto (store-bought or homemade)
- 2 tablespoons extra virgin olive oil
- 2 cloves garlic, minced
- Salt and pepper to taste
- Grated Parmesan cheese for serving (optional)

Instructions:

1. Using a spiralizer or vegetable peeler, spiralize or julienne the zucchinis into noodle-like strands. Set aside.
2. Heat the olive oil in a large skillet over medium heat. Add the minced garlic and sauté for about 1 minute until fragrant.
3. Add the zucchini noodles to the skillet and toss to coat them in the garlic-infused oil. Cook for 2-3 minutes, stirring occasionally, until the zucchini noodles are just tender but still have a slight crunch.
4. Add the cherry tomatoes to the skillet and cook for another 1-2 minutes until they are heated through but still slightly firm.
5. Remove the skillet from the heat and add the basil pesto to the zucchini noodles and cherry tomatoes. Toss everything together until the zucchini noodles and tomatoes are evenly coated with the pesto.
6. Taste and season with salt and pepper as needed.
7. Divide the zucchini noodles and cherry tomatoes among serving plates.
8. If desired, sprinkle grated Parmesan cheese over the top of each serving.
9. Serve immediately as a light and flavorful vegetarian main dish or as a side dish alongside grilled chicken or fish.

This dish is not only delicious but also low-carb and gluten-free, making it a healthy alternative to traditional pasta dishes. Enjoy the fresh flavors of summer with this Zucchini Noodles with Pesto and Cherry Tomatoes recipe!

Stuffed Bell Peppers with Quinoa and Kale

Ingredients:

- 4 large bell peppers (any color), tops cut off and seeds removed
- 1 cup quinoa, rinsed
- 2 cups vegetable broth or water
- 1 tablespoon olive oil
- 1 small onion, finely chopped
- 2 cloves garlic, minced
- 2 cups chopped kale (stems removed)
- 1 can (15 ounces) black beans, rinsed and drained
- 1 can (14.5 ounces) diced tomatoes, drained
- 1 teaspoon ground cumin
- 1 teaspoon smoked paprika
- Salt and pepper to taste
- Optional toppings: shredded cheese, avocado slices, chopped cilantro, hot sauce

Instructions:

1. Preheat the oven to 375°F (190°C).
2. In a medium saucepan, combine the quinoa and vegetable broth or water. Bring to a boil, then reduce the heat to low, cover, and simmer for about 15 minutes, or until the quinoa is cooked and the liquid is absorbed. Remove from heat and set aside.
3. While the quinoa is cooking, heat the olive oil in a large skillet over medium heat. Add the chopped onion and cook for 3-4 minutes until softened.
4. Add the minced garlic to the skillet and cook for another minute until fragrant.
5. Stir in the chopped kale and cook for 2-3 minutes until wilted.
6. Add the cooked quinoa, black beans, diced tomatoes, ground cumin, smoked paprika, salt, and pepper to the skillet. Stir to combine and cook for another 2-3 minutes until heated through.
7. Taste and adjust the seasoning if needed.
8. Stuff each bell pepper with the quinoa and kale mixture, pressing down gently to pack the filling.
9. Place the stuffed bell peppers in a baking dish, standing upright.
10. Cover the baking dish with foil and bake in the preheated oven for 25-30 minutes, or until the peppers are tender.

11. Remove the foil and optionally sprinkle shredded cheese over the tops of the stuffed peppers. Return to the oven and bake for an additional 5 minutes, or until the cheese is melted and bubbly.
12. Remove from the oven and let cool slightly before serving.
13. Garnish with avocado slices, chopped cilantro, and a drizzle of hot sauce, if desired.
14. Serve the stuffed bell peppers hot as a satisfying and nutritious vegetarian main dish.

These Stuffed Bell Peppers with Quinoa and Kale are packed with protein, fiber, and vitamins, making them a healthy and delicious meal option for lunch or dinner. Enjoy!

Roasted Beet and Goat Cheese Salad with Walnuts

Ingredients:

- 4 medium beets, washed and trimmed
- 4 ounces goat cheese, crumbled
- 1/2 cup walnuts, toasted and chopped
- 4 cups mixed salad greens (such as baby spinach, arugula, or spring mix)
- 2 tablespoons balsamic vinegar
- 2 tablespoons extra virgin olive oil
- Salt and pepper to taste

Instructions:

1. Preheat the oven to 400°F (200°C).
2. Wrap each beet individually in aluminum foil and place them on a baking sheet. Roast in the preheated oven for 45-60 minutes, or until the beets are tender when pierced with a fork.
3. Once the beets are roasted and cooled slightly, peel off the skins using a paper towel or wear gloves to prevent staining your hands. Cut the beets into wedges or slices.
4. In a small bowl, whisk together the balsamic vinegar, extra virgin olive oil, salt, and pepper to make the dressing.
5. In a large mixing bowl, combine the mixed salad greens with the roasted beet slices.
6. Drizzle the dressing over the salad and toss to coat evenly.
7. Divide the dressed salad greens and beets among serving plates.
8. Sprinkle crumbled goat cheese and chopped walnuts over the top of each salad.
9. Serve immediately as a refreshing and flavorful appetizer or side dish.

This Roasted Beet and Goat Cheese Salad with Walnuts is not only visually stunning but also packed with nutrients and flavors. Enjoy the combination of sweet roasted beets, tangy goat cheese, crunchy walnuts, and crisp salad greens in every bite!

Vegetable Stir-Fry with Tofu or Chicken

Ingredients:

- 1 block (14 oz) firm tofu OR 2 boneless, skinless chicken breasts, thinly sliced
- 2 tablespoons soy sauce (or tamari for gluten-free option)
- 2 tablespoons rice vinegar
- 1 tablespoon sesame oil
- 1 tablespoon cornstarch
- 2 tablespoons vegetable oil, divided
- 3 cloves garlic, minced
- 1 tablespoon fresh ginger, minced
- Assorted vegetables, chopped (such as bell peppers, broccoli, carrots, snap peas, mushrooms, onions, and zucchini)
- Cooked rice or noodles for serving
- Optional garnishes: sesame seeds, chopped green onions, sliced red chili

Instructions:

1. If using tofu, drain the tofu and wrap it in a clean kitchen towel or paper towels. Place a heavy object (like a plate or skillet) on top to press out excess water for about 15-20 minutes. Then cut the tofu into cubes.
2. In a small bowl, mix together the soy sauce, rice vinegar, sesame oil, and cornstarch. Set aside.
3. Heat 1 tablespoon of vegetable oil in a large skillet or wok over medium-high heat. Add the tofu cubes or sliced chicken to the skillet and cook until golden brown and cooked through. If using tofu, it may take about 5-7 minutes per side. If using chicken, it may take about 4-5 minutes per side. Once cooked, remove from the skillet and set aside.
4. In the same skillet, add the remaining tablespoon of vegetable oil. Add the minced garlic and ginger, and sauté for about 1 minute until fragrant.
5. Add the chopped vegetables to the skillet and stir-fry for 5-7 minutes, or until they are crisp-tender.
6. Return the cooked tofu or chicken to the skillet with the vegetables.
7. Pour the sauce mixture over the tofu/chicken and vegetables in the skillet. Stir well to coat everything evenly.

8. Continue cooking for another 2-3 minutes, or until the sauce has thickened and everything is heated through.
9. Taste and adjust seasoning if needed.
10. Serve the vegetable stir-fry hot over cooked rice or noodles.
11. Garnish with sesame seeds, chopped green onions, and sliced red chili if desired.
12. Enjoy your delicious and nutritious Vegetable Stir-Fry with Tofu or Chicken!

This recipe is easily customizable based on your preferences and what vegetables you have on hand. It's a quick, healthy, and satisfying meal option for any day of the week!

Butternut Squash Soup with Apple and Sage

Ingredients:

- 1 medium butternut squash, peeled, seeded, and diced (about 4 cups)
- 1 large apple, peeled, cored, and diced
- 1 onion, diced
- 2 cloves garlic, minced
- 4 cups vegetable or chicken broth
- 1/2 teaspoon ground cinnamon
- 1/4 teaspoon ground nutmeg
- 1/4 teaspoon ground ginger
- 1/2 cup heavy cream (optional)
- Salt and pepper to taste
- Fresh sage leaves for garnish
- Olive oil for cooking

Instructions:

1. Heat a large pot over medium heat and add a drizzle of olive oil.
2. Add the diced onion to the pot and cook for 3-4 minutes until softened.
3. Add the minced garlic to the pot and cook for another minute until fragrant.
4. Add the diced butternut squash, diced apple, ground cinnamon, ground nutmeg, and ground ginger to the pot. Stir to combine.
5. Pour the vegetable or chicken broth into the pot, ensuring that the vegetables are mostly covered by the broth.
6. Bring the mixture to a boil, then reduce the heat to low and simmer for about 20-25 minutes, or until the butternut squash and apple are tender.
7. Use an immersion blender to puree the soup until smooth and creamy. Alternatively, carefully transfer the soup in batches to a blender and blend until smooth, then return it to the pot.
8. If using, stir in the heavy cream to add richness to the soup.
9. Taste and adjust the seasoning with salt and pepper as needed.
10. Ladle the soup into bowls and garnish each serving with fresh sage leaves.
11. Serve the Butternut Squash Soup hot, alongside crusty bread or a green salad.

This Butternut Squash Soup with Apple and Sage is both comforting and flavorful, making it perfect for chilly days or as a starter for a special meal. Enjoy the delightful combination of sweet butternut squash, tart apple, and aromatic sage!

Fresh Tomato Bruschetta with Basil

Ingredients:

- 4-5 ripe tomatoes, diced
- 2 cloves garlic, minced
- 1/4 cup fresh basil leaves, chopped
- 2 tablespoons extra virgin olive oil
- 1 tablespoon balsamic vinegar (optional)
- Salt and pepper to taste
- 1 baguette or Italian bread, sliced
- Olive oil for brushing

Instructions:

1. In a mixing bowl, combine the diced tomatoes, minced garlic, chopped basil leaves, extra virgin olive oil, and balsamic vinegar (if using). Mix well to combine.
2. Season the tomato mixture with salt and pepper to taste. Set aside to allow the flavors to meld together while you prepare the bread.
3. Preheat your oven to 375°F (190°C).
4. Arrange the sliced baguette or Italian bread on a baking sheet in a single layer.
5. Brush each slice of bread lightly with olive oil on one side.
6. Place the baking sheet in the preheated oven and bake for 8-10 minutes, or until the bread slices are golden brown and crisp.
7. Remove the toasted bread from the oven and let it cool slightly.
8. Once cooled, spoon the tomato mixture generously onto each toasted bread slice.
9. Arrange the bruschetta on a serving platter and garnish with additional fresh basil leaves if desired.
10. Serve the Fresh Tomato Bruschetta with Basil immediately as an appetizer or light snack.

This Fresh Tomato Bruschetta with Basil is bursting with the flavors of ripe tomatoes and fragrant basil, making it a perfect dish to enjoy during the summer months or as a starter for any meal. Enjoy the simplicity and freshness of this classic Italian appetizer!

Spinach and Feta Stuffed Mushrooms

Ingredients:

- 12 large mushrooms, cleaned and stems removed
- 2 tablespoons olive oil
- 2 cloves garlic, minced
- 2 cups fresh spinach, chopped
- 1/2 cup crumbled feta cheese
- 1/4 cup grated Parmesan cheese
- Salt and pepper to taste
- 1 tablespoon chopped fresh parsley (optional, for garnish)

Instructions:

1. Preheat your oven to 375°F (190°C).
2. Heat the olive oil in a large skillet over medium heat. Add the minced garlic and cook for 1-2 minutes until fragrant.
3. Add the chopped spinach to the skillet and cook for 2-3 minutes until wilted. Remove from heat and let cool slightly.
4. In a mixing bowl, combine the cooked spinach with the crumbled feta cheese, grated Parmesan cheese, salt, and pepper. Mix well to combine.
5. Spoon the spinach and feta mixture into each mushroom cap, filling them generously.
6. Place the stuffed mushrooms on a baking sheet lined with parchment paper or aluminum foil.
7. Bake in the preheated oven for 15-20 minutes, or until the mushrooms are tender and the filling is golden brown and bubbly.
8. Remove from the oven and let cool for a few minutes before serving.
9. Garnish with chopped fresh parsley, if desired, before serving.

These Spinach and Feta Stuffed Mushrooms are perfect as an appetizer for parties or as a flavorful side dish for any meal. Enjoy the combination of earthy mushrooms, savory spinach, and tangy feta cheese in every bite!

Grilled Eggplant with Tahini Sauce

Ingredients:

- 1 large eggplant, sliced into 1/2-inch rounds
- Salt
- Olive oil for brushing
- Fresh parsley or cilantro for garnish

For the Tahini Sauce:

- 1/4 cup tahini (sesame seed paste)
- 2 tablespoons lemon juice
- 1 clove garlic, minced
- 2-4 tablespoons water (to adjust consistency)
- Salt and pepper to taste

Instructions:

1. Start by preparing the eggplant. Lay the eggplant slices on a baking sheet or large plate and sprinkle both sides generously with salt. Let them sit for about 20-30 minutes to draw out excess moisture and bitterness.
2. While the eggplant is resting, preheat your grill to medium-high heat.
3. After the resting period, use paper towels to blot excess moisture and salt from the eggplant slices.
4. Brush both sides of the eggplant slices with olive oil to prevent sticking on the grill.
5. Grill the eggplant slices for about 4-5 minutes per side, or until tender and grill marks appear. Cooking time may vary depending on the thickness of the slices and the heat of your grill.
6. While the eggplant is grilling, prepare the tahini sauce. In a small bowl, whisk together the tahini, lemon juice, minced garlic, and a pinch of salt and pepper. Gradually add water, one tablespoon at a time, until you reach your desired consistency. The sauce should be smooth and pourable.
7. Once the eggplant slices are grilled to your liking, remove them from the grill and arrange them on a serving platter.
8. Drizzle the tahini sauce over the grilled eggplant slices.

9. Garnish with fresh parsley or cilantro.
10. Serve the Grilled Eggplant with Tahini Sauce as a delicious appetizer or side dish.

This dish offers a wonderful combination of smoky grilled eggplant with creamy tahini sauce, creating a flavorful and satisfying dish that's perfect for summer gatherings or any time you're craving a healthy and delicious meal. Enjoy!

Summer Squash and Corn Chowder

Ingredients:

- 4 ears of fresh corn, husked and kernels removed (or 3 cups frozen corn kernels)
- 2 tablespoons olive oil
- 1 onion, chopped
- 2 cloves garlic, minced
- 2 medium summer squash (such as yellow squash or zucchini), diced
- 1 large potato, peeled and diced
- 4 cups vegetable or chicken broth
- 1 cup milk or cream
- Salt and pepper to taste
- 1/4 cup chopped fresh parsley or cilantro (optional, for garnish)
- Crumbled bacon or cooked diced chicken (optional, for added protein)

Instructions:

1. Heat the olive oil in a large pot over medium heat. Add the chopped onion and cook for 3-4 minutes until softened.
2. Add the minced garlic to the pot and cook for another minute until fragrant.
3. Add the diced summer squash and potato to the pot. Cook for 5-7 minutes, stirring occasionally, until the vegetables start to soften.
4. Add the fresh corn kernels to the pot. If using frozen corn, you can add it directly from the freezer. Cook for another 3-4 minutes.
5. Pour the vegetable or chicken broth into the pot, ensuring that the vegetables are mostly covered by the liquid. Bring the mixture to a boil.
6. Once boiling, reduce the heat to low and simmer the chowder for about 15-20 minutes, or until the vegetables are tender.
7. Using an immersion blender or regular blender, carefully puree about half of the chowder until smooth. This helps thicken the chowder while still leaving some texture.
8. Stir in the milk or cream, and season with salt and pepper to taste. If the chowder is too thick, you can add more broth or milk to reach your desired consistency.
9. If using, stir in the crumbled bacon or cooked diced chicken for added flavor and protein.
10. Ladle the Summer Squash and Corn Chowder into bowls and garnish with chopped fresh parsley or cilantro, if desired.

11. Serve the chowder hot, accompanied by crusty bread or crackers.

This Summer Squash and Corn Chowder is creamy, flavorful, and perfect for using up an abundance of summer produce. Enjoy the delicious combination of sweet corn, tender squash, and savory broth in every spoonful!

Kale and White Bean Soup

Ingredients:

- 2 tablespoons olive oil
- 1 onion, chopped
- 2 cloves garlic, minced
- 2 carrots, diced
- 2 celery stalks, diced
- 1 teaspoon dried thyme
- 1 teaspoon dried oregano
- 1/2 teaspoon smoked paprika
- 6 cups vegetable or chicken broth
- 2 cans (15 ounces each) white beans (such as cannellini beans), drained and rinsed
- 1 bunch kale, stems removed and leaves chopped
- Salt and pepper to taste
- Grated Parmesan cheese for serving (optional)
- Crusty bread for serving (optional)

Instructions:

1. Heat the olive oil in a large pot over medium heat. Add the chopped onion and cook for 3-4 minutes until softened.
2. Add the minced garlic to the pot and cook for another minute until fragrant.
3. Add the diced carrots and celery to the pot. Cook for 5-7 minutes, stirring occasionally, until the vegetables start to soften.
4. Stir in the dried thyme, dried oregano, and smoked paprika, and cook for another minute until fragrant.
5. Pour the vegetable or chicken broth into the pot, scraping up any browned bits from the bottom. Bring the mixture to a boil.
6. Once boiling, reduce the heat to low and simmer the soup for about 15-20 minutes, or until the vegetables are tender.
7. Add the drained and rinsed white beans to the pot. Stir well to combine.
8. Add the chopped kale to the pot, a handful at a time, stirring until wilted.
9. Simmer the soup for another 5-10 minutes to allow the flavors to meld together and the kale to soften.

10. Taste and season the soup with salt and pepper to taste.
11. Ladle the Kale and White Bean Soup into bowls and serve hot.
12. If desired, garnish each serving with grated Parmesan cheese and serve with crusty bread on the side.

This Kale and White Bean Soup is hearty, nutritious, and perfect for chilly days. Enjoy the comforting combination of tender vegetables, creamy beans, and flavorful broth in every spoonful!

Roasted Garlic and Tomato Pasta

Ingredients:

- 1 head of garlic
- 2 tablespoons olive oil, divided
- 1 pound cherry tomatoes
- Salt and pepper to taste
- 8 ounces pasta (such as spaghetti, penne, or linguine)
- Fresh basil leaves, chopped (for garnish)
- Grated Parmesan cheese (optional, for serving)

Instructions:

1. Preheat your oven to 400°F (200°C).
2. Cut the top off the head of garlic to expose the cloves. Place the garlic head on a piece of aluminum foil, drizzle with 1 tablespoon of olive oil, and wrap it up in the foil.
3. Place the foil-wrapped garlic on a baking sheet along with the cherry tomatoes. Drizzle the tomatoes with the remaining tablespoon of olive oil and season with salt and pepper to taste.
4. Roast the garlic and tomatoes in the preheated oven for 25-30 minutes, or until the garlic cloves are soft and caramelized, and the tomatoes are bursting and juicy.
5. While the garlic and tomatoes are roasting, cook the pasta according to the package instructions until al dente. Drain, reserving a cup of pasta cooking water.
6. Once the garlic and tomatoes are roasted, remove them from the oven. Squeeze the roasted garlic cloves out of their skins and mash them into a paste.
7. In a large skillet, heat a tablespoon of olive oil over medium heat. Add the roasted garlic paste and cook for 1-2 minutes until fragrant.
8. Add the roasted cherry tomatoes to the skillet, along with any juices from the baking sheet. Cook for another 2-3 minutes, breaking up the tomatoes slightly with a spoon.
9. Add the cooked pasta to the skillet, tossing to coat it in the garlic and tomato mixture. If the sauce seems too thick, you can add a splash of pasta cooking water to loosen it up.
10. Taste and adjust the seasoning with salt and pepper as needed.

11. Serve the Roasted Garlic and Tomato Pasta hot, garnished with chopped fresh basil leaves and grated Parmesan cheese if desired.

This Roasted Garlic and Tomato Pasta is bursting with flavor from the sweet roasted tomatoes and caramelized garlic, making it a simple yet satisfying meal that's perfect for any night of the week. Enjoy!

Cucumber Salad with Dill and Greek Yogurt Dressing

Ingredients:

- 2 large cucumbers, thinly sliced
- 1/4 cup red onion, thinly sliced
- 1/4 cup fresh dill, chopped
- 1/2 cup Greek yogurt
- 1 tablespoon lemon juice
- 1 tablespoon extra virgin olive oil
- 1 clove garlic, minced
- Salt and pepper to taste

Instructions:

1. In a large mixing bowl, combine the thinly sliced cucumbers, red onion slices, and chopped fresh dill.
2. In a separate small bowl, whisk together the Greek yogurt, lemon juice, extra virgin olive oil, minced garlic, salt, and pepper to make the dressing.
3. Pour the dressing over the cucumber mixture in the large mixing bowl.
4. Toss everything together until the cucumbers and onions are evenly coated with the dressing.
5. Taste and adjust the seasoning with salt and pepper as needed.
6. Cover the bowl and refrigerate the cucumber salad for at least 30 minutes to allow the flavors to meld together and the salad to chill.
7. Before serving, give the salad a final toss and garnish with a sprig of fresh dill if desired.
8. Serve the Cucumber Salad with Dill and Greek Yogurt Dressing cold as a refreshing side dish or light appetizer.

This salad is light, crisp, and packed with fresh flavors from the cucumbers, dill, and tangy Greek yogurt dressing. It's perfect for picnics, barbecues, or as a healthy addition to any meal. Enjoy!

Roasted Carrots with Honey and Thyme

Ingredients:

- 1 pound carrots, peeled and trimmed
- 2 tablespoons olive oil
- 2 tablespoons honey
- 2-3 sprigs fresh thyme (or 1 teaspoon dried thyme)
- Salt and pepper to taste
- Chopped fresh parsley for garnish (optional)

Instructions:

1. Preheat your oven to 400°F (200°C).
2. Cut the carrots into uniform pieces, about 2-3 inches long.
3. In a mixing bowl, combine the olive oil, honey, and leaves from the thyme sprigs. If using dried thyme, add it to the mixture as well. Stir until well combined.
4. Add the carrots to the bowl and toss to coat them evenly with the honey and thyme mixture.
5. Arrange the coated carrots in a single layer on a baking sheet lined with parchment paper or aluminum foil.
6. Season the carrots with salt and pepper to taste.
7. Roast the carrots in the preheated oven for 20-25 minutes, or until they are tender and caramelized, stirring halfway through the cooking time to ensure even roasting.
8. Once roasted, remove the carrots from the oven and transfer them to a serving platter.
9. Garnish the roasted carrots with chopped fresh parsley, if desired.
10. Serve the Roasted Carrots with Honey and Thyme hot as a flavorful side dish.

These Roasted Carrots with Honey and Thyme are sweet, savory, and aromatic, making them a perfect accompaniment to any meal. Enjoy the delicious combination of caramelized carrots, fragrant thyme, and a touch of sweetness from the honey!

Panzanella Salad with Cucumber, Tomato, and Bread

Ingredients:

- 4 cups stale bread, cubed (such as ciabatta or sourdough)
- 2 large tomatoes, diced
- 1 cucumber, diced
- 1/2 red onion, thinly sliced
- 1/4 cup fresh basil leaves, torn
- 1/4 cup fresh parsley leaves, chopped
- 1/4 cup extra virgin olive oil
- 2 tablespoons red wine vinegar
- 1 clove garlic, minced
- Salt and pepper to taste

Instructions:

1. Preheat your oven to 375°F (190°C).
2. Spread the cubed stale bread on a baking sheet in a single layer. Bake in the preheated oven for about 10-15 minutes, or until the bread cubes are crisp and golden brown. Remove from the oven and let cool.
3. In a large mixing bowl, combine the diced tomatoes, diced cucumber, thinly sliced red onion, torn basil leaves, and chopped parsley leaves.
4. In a small bowl, whisk together the extra virgin olive oil, red wine vinegar, minced garlic, salt, and pepper to make the dressing.
5. Pour the dressing over the tomato, cucumber, and bread mixture in the large mixing bowl. Toss everything together until well coated.
6. Add the toasted bread cubes to the salad and toss again gently to combine.
7. Let the Panzanella Salad sit for about 10-15 minutes before serving, allowing the flavors to meld together and the bread to soak up the dressing.
8. Taste and adjust the seasoning with salt and pepper if needed.
9. Serve the Panzanella Salad with Cucumber, Tomato, and Bread as a refreshing appetizer or side dish.

This Panzanella Salad is a classic Italian dish that celebrates the flavors of summer with ripe tomatoes, crisp cucumbers, fragrant basil, and crunchy bread. Enjoy the vibrant colors and fresh taste of this delicious salad!

Sweet Potato and Black Bean Enchiladas

Ingredients:

- 2 large sweet potatoes, peeled and diced
- 1 can (15 ounces) black beans, drained and rinsed
- 1 small onion, diced
- 2 cloves garlic, minced
- 1 teaspoon ground cumin
- 1 teaspoon chili powder
- 1/2 teaspoon paprika
- Salt and pepper to taste
- 1 cup shredded cheese (such as cheddar or Mexican blend)
- 8-10 small flour or corn tortillas
- Enchilada sauce (store-bought or homemade)
- Chopped fresh cilantro, for garnish
- Sour cream or Greek yogurt, for serving (optional)
- Sliced avocado, for serving (optional)

Instructions:

1. Preheat your oven to 375°F (190°C).
2. Place the diced sweet potatoes in a microwave-safe bowl and microwave for 5-7 minutes, or until they are tender.
3. In a large skillet, heat a bit of olive oil over medium heat. Add the diced onion and cook until translucent, about 3-4 minutes.
4. Add the minced garlic to the skillet and cook for another minute until fragrant.
5. Add the cooked sweet potatoes, black beans, ground cumin, chili powder, paprika, salt, and pepper to the skillet. Stir to combine and cook for a few minutes until heated through.
6. Warm the tortillas slightly to make them pliable. You can do this in the microwave or on a hot skillet for a few seconds on each side.
7. Spread a spoonful of enchilada sauce on the bottom of a baking dish.
8. Place a spoonful of the sweet potato and black bean mixture in the center of each tortilla. Roll up the tortillas and place them seam-side down in the baking dish.

9. Once all the enchiladas are assembled in the baking dish, pour the remaining enchilada sauce over the top, covering them evenly.
10. Sprinkle shredded cheese over the top of the enchiladas.
11. Cover the baking dish with aluminum foil and bake in the preheated oven for 20-25 minutes, or until the cheese is melted and bubbly.
12. Remove the foil and bake for an additional 5 minutes to allow the cheese to brown slightly.
13. Once baked, remove the enchiladas from the oven and let them cool slightly before serving.
14. Garnish with chopped fresh cilantro and serve with sour cream or Greek yogurt and sliced avocado, if desired.

These Sweet Potato and Black Bean Enchiladas are a flavorful and satisfying vegetarian dish that's perfect for a cozy dinner. Enjoy the combination of sweet potatoes, black beans, and spices wrapped in warm tortillas and topped with enchilada sauce and cheese!

Spinach and Mushroom Quiche

Ingredients:

- 1 pie crust (store-bought or homemade)
- 1 tablespoon olive oil
- 1 small onion, finely chopped
- 8 ounces mushrooms, sliced
- 2 cloves garlic, minced
- 2 cups fresh spinach, chopped
- 4 large eggs
- 1 cup milk (or half-and-half for a richer quiche)
- 1 cup shredded cheese (such as Swiss, Gruyere, or cheddar)
- Salt and pepper to taste
- Pinch of nutmeg (optional)
- Chopped fresh parsley or thyme for garnish (optional)

Instructions:

1. Preheat your oven to 375°F (190°C).
2. Roll out the pie crust and press it into a 9-inch pie dish. Crimp the edges of the crust as desired.
3. Heat the olive oil in a large skillet over medium heat. Add the chopped onion and cook for 3-4 minutes until softened.
4. Add the sliced mushrooms to the skillet and cook for 5-6 minutes until they release their moisture and start to brown.
5. Add the minced garlic to the skillet and cook for another minute until fragrant.
6. Stir in the chopped spinach and cook for 2-3 minutes until wilted. Remove from heat and let the mixture cool slightly.
7. In a mixing bowl, whisk together the eggs and milk until well combined. Season with salt, pepper, and a pinch of nutmeg if using.
8. Spread the mushroom and spinach mixture evenly over the bottom of the pie crust.
9. Sprinkle shredded cheese over the top of the mushroom and spinach mixture.
10. Pour the egg and milk mixture over the filling in the pie crust.
11. Gently tap the pie dish on the counter to release any air bubbles.

12. Place the quiche in the preheated oven and bake for 35-40 minutes, or until the center is set and the top is golden brown.
13. Remove the quiche from the oven and let it cool for a few minutes before slicing.
14. Garnish with chopped fresh parsley or thyme, if desired.
15. Serve the Spinach and Mushroom Quiche warm or at room temperature.

This Spinach and Mushroom Quiche is perfect for brunch, lunch, or a light dinner. It's flavorful, satisfying, and versatile, making it a great option for any occasion! Enjoy!

Grilled Portobello Mushrooms with Balsamic Glaze

Ingredients:

- 1 pie crust (store-bought or homemade)
- 1 tablespoon olive oil
- 1 small onion, finely chopped
- 8 ounces mushrooms, sliced
- 2 cloves garlic, minced
- 2 cups fresh spinach, chopped
- 4 large eggs
- 1 cup milk (or half-and-half for a richer quiche)
- 1 cup shredded cheese (such as Swiss, Gruyere, or cheddar)
- Salt and pepper to taste
- Pinch of nutmeg (optional)
- Chopped fresh parsley or thyme for garnish (optional)

Instructions:

1. Preheat your oven to 375°F (190°C).
2. Roll out the pie crust and press it into a 9-inch pie dish. Crimp the edges of the crust as desired.
3. Heat the olive oil in a large skillet over medium heat. Add the chopped onion and cook for 3-4 minutes until softened.
4. Add the sliced mushrooms to the skillet and cook for 5-6 minutes until they release their moisture and start to brown.
5. Add the minced garlic to the skillet and cook for another minute until fragrant.
6. Stir in the chopped spinach and cook for 2-3 minutes until wilted. Remove from heat and let the mixture cool slightly.
7. In a mixing bowl, whisk together the eggs and milk until well combined. Season with salt, pepper, and a pinch of nutmeg if using.
8. Spread the mushroom and spinach mixture evenly over the bottom of the pie crust.
9. Sprinkle shredded cheese over the top of the mushroom and spinach mixture.
10. Pour the egg and milk mixture over the filling in the pie crust.
11. Gently tap the pie dish on the counter to release any air bubbles.

12. Place the quiche in the preheated oven and bake for 35-40 minutes, or until the center is set and the top is golden brown.
13. Remove the quiche from the oven and let it cool for a few minutes before slicing.
14. Garnish with chopped fresh parsley or thyme, if desired.
15. Serve the Spinach and Mushroom Quiche warm or at room temperature.

This Spinach and Mushroom Quiche is perfect for brunch, lunch, or a light dinner. It's flavorful, satisfying, and versatile, making it a great option for any occasion! Enjoy!

Asparagus and Goat Cheese Tart

Ingredients:

- 1 sheet puff pastry, thawed if frozen
- 1 bunch asparagus, tough ends trimmed
- 4 ounces goat cheese, crumbled
- 2 tablespoons grated Parmesan cheese
- 2 tablespoons olive oil
- 2 cloves garlic, minced
- Salt and pepper to taste
- Fresh thyme leaves for garnish (optional)

Instructions:

1. Preheat your oven to 400°F (200°C).
2. Roll out the puff pastry on a lightly floured surface to fit a baking sheet or tart pan. Place the rolled-out pastry onto the baking sheet or tart pan.
3. Use a fork to prick holes in the bottom of the pastry to prevent it from puffing up too much during baking.
4. In a small bowl, mix together the olive oil and minced garlic.
5. Brush the garlic-infused olive oil over the surface of the pastry.
6. Sprinkle the crumbled goat cheese evenly over the pastry, leaving a border around the edges.
7. Arrange the trimmed asparagus spears on top of the goat cheese, alternating the direction of the spears if desired.
8. Sprinkle grated Parmesan cheese over the asparagus.
9. Season the tart with salt and pepper to taste.
10. Place the tart in the preheated oven and bake for 20-25 minutes, or until the pastry is golden brown and the asparagus is tender.
11. Once baked, remove the tart from the oven and let it cool slightly before serving.
12. Garnish with fresh thyme leaves, if desired.
13. Slice the Asparagus and Goat Cheese Tart into portions and serve warm or at room temperature.

This Asparagus and Goat Cheese Tart is a delightful combination of buttery puff pastry, creamy goat cheese, and tender asparagus. It's perfect for brunch, lunch, or as an appetizer for a special occasion. Enjoy the delicious flavors and elegant presentation of this tart!

Roasted Cauliflower with Lemon and Parmesan

Ingredients:

- 1 head cauliflower, cut into florets
- 2 tablespoons olive oil
- Zest of 1 lemon
- Juice of 1/2 lemon
- 1/4 cup grated Parmesan cheese
- 2 cloves garlic, minced
- Salt and pepper to taste
- Fresh parsley, chopped, for garnish (optional)

Instructions:

1. Preheat your oven to 425°F (220°C).
2. In a large mixing bowl, toss the cauliflower florets with olive oil, lemon zest, lemon juice, grated Parmesan cheese, minced garlic, salt, and pepper until evenly coated.
3. Spread the cauliflower in a single layer on a baking sheet lined with parchment paper or aluminum foil.
4. Roast in the preheated oven for 25-30 minutes, or until the cauliflower is tender and golden brown, stirring halfway through the cooking time for even roasting.
5. Once roasted, remove the cauliflower from the oven and transfer it to a serving dish.
6. Garnish with chopped fresh parsley, if desired, before serving.
7. Serve the Roasted Cauliflower with Lemon and Parmesan hot as a flavorful side dish or appetizer.

This Roasted Cauliflower with Lemon and Parmesan is bursting with flavor from the tangy lemon zest, nutty Parmesan cheese, and caramelized cauliflower. It's a simple yet satisfying dish that pairs well with a variety of main courses. Enjoy the deliciousness!

Fresh Pea Risotto with Mint

Ingredients:

- 1 cup Arborio rice
- 3 cups vegetable or chicken broth, kept warm
- 1 cup fresh peas (or frozen peas, thawed)
- 1 small onion, finely chopped
- 2 cloves garlic, minced
- 1/2 cup dry white wine
- 2 tablespoons unsalted butter
- 1/4 cup grated Parmesan cheese
- 2 tablespoons fresh mint leaves, chopped
- Salt and pepper to taste
- Extra virgin olive oil for drizzling (optional)
- Fresh mint leaves for garnish (optional)

Instructions:

1. In a saucepan, heat the vegetable or chicken broth over low heat and keep it warm.
2. In a separate large skillet or pot, melt 1 tablespoon of butter over medium heat. Add the chopped onion and cook until softened, about 3-4 minutes.
3. Add the minced garlic to the skillet and cook for another minute until fragrant.
4. Add the Arborio rice to the skillet and stir to coat it with the butter, onion, and garlic mixture. Cook for 1-2 minutes until the rice is lightly toasted.
5. Pour in the dry white wine and stir until it is absorbed by the rice.
6. Begin adding the warm broth to the rice mixture, one ladleful at a time, stirring frequently. Allow each addition of broth to be absorbed by the rice before adding more. Continue this process until the rice is creamy and cooked to al dente texture, about 18-20 minutes.
7. Stir in the fresh peas during the last few minutes of cooking, allowing them to cook until tender.
8. Once the risotto is cooked to your desired consistency, remove it from the heat and stir in the remaining tablespoon of butter, grated Parmesan cheese, and chopped fresh mint leaves. Season with salt and pepper to taste.
9. Serve the Fresh Pea Risotto with Mint hot, drizzled with extra virgin olive oil and garnished with fresh mint leaves if desired.

This Fresh Pea Risotto with Mint is creamy, flavorful, and showcases the vibrant flavors of spring. Enjoy the combination of tender Arborio rice, sweet peas, and fragrant mint in every spoonful!

Grilled Corn on the Cob with Herb Butter

Ingredients:

- 4 ears of corn, husked
- 4 tablespoons unsalted butter, softened
- 2 tablespoons mixed fresh herbs (such as parsley, chives, thyme, or basil), finely chopped
- 1 clove garlic, minced (optional)
- Salt and pepper to taste

Instructions:

1. Preheat your grill to medium-high heat.
2. In a small bowl, combine the softened butter, chopped fresh herbs, minced garlic (if using), salt, and pepper. Mix until well combined.
3. Place each ear of corn on a piece of aluminum foil.
4. Spread a generous amount of the herb butter mixture over each ear of corn, making sure to coat it evenly.
5. Wrap the foil around the corn to form packets, ensuring they are sealed tightly.
6. Place the foil-wrapped corn directly on the grill grate.
7. Grill the corn for about 15-20 minutes, turning occasionally, until the kernels are tender and lightly charred.
8. Carefully remove the foil-wrapped corn from the grill and let them cool for a few minutes.
9. Unwrap the corn from the foil packets and serve hot.
10. Optionally, you can brush the grilled corn with any remaining herb butter before serving for an extra burst of flavor.

This Grilled Corn on the Cob with Herb Butter is a perfect side dish for summer cookouts and gatherings. The combination of sweet, smoky corn and savory herb butter is irresistible! Enjoy the deliciousness!

Rainbow Chard and White Bean Saute

Ingredients:

- 1 bunch rainbow chard
- 1 can (15 ounces) white beans (such as cannellini or Great Northern), drained and rinsed
- 2 tablespoons olive oil
- 2 cloves garlic, minced
- 1 small onion, finely chopped
- Salt and pepper to taste
- Pinch of red pepper flakes (optional)
- Juice of 1/2 lemon
- Grated Parmesan cheese for serving (optional)

Instructions:

1. Wash the rainbow chard thoroughly under cold water. Remove the tough stems and chop the leaves into bite-sized pieces. Keep the stems and leaves separate.
2. Heat the olive oil in a large skillet over medium heat. Add the minced garlic and chopped onion to the skillet and cook for 2-3 minutes until softened and fragrant.
3. Add the chopped chard stems to the skillet and cook for 4-5 minutes until they begin to soften.
4. Add the chopped chard leaves to the skillet in batches, allowing them to wilt down before adding more. Cook for 3-4 minutes until all the chard leaves are wilted.
5. Stir in the drained and rinsed white beans, salt, pepper, and a pinch of red pepper flakes if using. Cook for another 2-3 minutes until heated through.
6. Squeeze the lemon juice over the saute and stir to combine.
7. Taste and adjust the seasoning if needed.
8. Remove the skillet from heat and transfer the Rainbow Chard and White Bean Saute to a serving dish.
9. Optionally, sprinkle grated Parmesan cheese over the top before serving.

This Rainbow Chard and White Bean Saute is a nutritious and flavorful dish that's quick and easy to prepare. Enjoy it as a vegetarian main dish or as a flavorful side to accompany any meal!

Tomato and Basil Galette

Ingredients:

For the crust:

- 1 1/4 cups all-purpose flour
- 1/2 teaspoon salt
- 8 tablespoons unsalted butter, cold and cut into small pieces
- 3-4 tablespoons ice water

For the filling:

- 2-3 large tomatoes, thinly sliced
- 1/4 cup fresh basil leaves, chopped
- 1/2 cup shredded mozzarella cheese
- 2 tablespoons grated Parmesan cheese
- 1 tablespoon olive oil
- Salt and pepper to taste
- 1 egg, beaten (for egg wash)
- Additional fresh basil leaves for garnish (optional)

Instructions:

1. Preheat your oven to 375°F (190°C).
2. To make the crust, in a large mixing bowl, combine the all-purpose flour and salt. Add the cold butter pieces and use a pastry cutter or your fingertips to work the butter into the flour until the mixture resembles coarse crumbs.
3. Gradually add the ice water, one tablespoon at a time, and mix until the dough comes together. Be careful not to overwork the dough. Shape the dough into a disk, wrap it in plastic wrap, and refrigerate for at least 30 minutes.
4. On a lightly floured surface, roll out the chilled dough into a rough circle, about 12 inches in diameter. Transfer the rolled-out dough to a parchment-lined baking sheet.

5. Arrange the thinly sliced tomatoes in the center of the dough, leaving a border around the edges. Sprinkle the chopped basil leaves over the tomatoes, followed by the shredded mozzarella and grated Parmesan cheese. Drizzle olive oil over the top and season with salt and pepper to taste.
6. Fold the edges of the dough up and over the filling, pleating as needed to create a rustic galette shape.
7. Brush the edges of the crust with beaten egg to create a golden brown finish.
8. Bake the Tomato and Basil Galette in the preheated oven for 30-35 minutes, or until the crust is golden brown and the filling is bubbly.
9. Once baked, remove the galette from the oven and let it cool for a few minutes before slicing.
10. Garnish with additional fresh basil leaves, if desired, before serving.

This Tomato and Basil Galette is a perfect way to showcase ripe summer tomatoes and fragrant basil. Enjoy the combination of flaky crust, juicy tomatoes, and savory cheese in every bite!

Beet and Carrot Salad with Citrus Dressing

Ingredients:

For the salad:

- 2 medium beets, peeled and grated
- 2 large carrots, peeled and grated
- 1/4 cup chopped fresh parsley or cilantro
- 1/4 cup toasted walnuts or pecans, chopped (optional)
- Salt and pepper to taste

For the citrus dressing:

- Juice of 1 orange
- Juice of 1 lemon
- 2 tablespoons extra virgin olive oil
- 1 teaspoon honey or maple syrup (optional)
- 1 teaspoon Dijon mustard
- Salt and pepper to taste

Instructions:

1. In a large mixing bowl, combine the grated beets, grated carrots, chopped fresh parsley or cilantro, and toasted walnuts or pecans (if using). Toss to combine.
2. In a small bowl, whisk together the orange juice, lemon juice, extra virgin olive oil, honey or maple syrup (if using), Dijon mustard, salt, and pepper to make the citrus dressing.
3. Pour the citrus dressing over the beet and carrot mixture in the large mixing bowl. Toss until the salad is evenly coated with the dressing.
4. Taste and adjust the seasoning with salt and pepper if needed.
5. Let the Beet and Carrot Salad marinate in the refrigerator for at least 30 minutes to allow the flavors to meld together.
6. Before serving, give the salad a final toss and adjust the seasoning if needed.
7. Serve the Beet and Carrot Salad with Citrus Dressing chilled, garnished with additional fresh herbs or nuts if desired.

This Beet and Carrot Salad with Citrus Dressing is a refreshing and vibrant dish that's bursting with flavor and color. Enjoy the crisp texture of the grated beets and carrots, complemented by the bright and tangy citrus dressing!

Broccoli and Cheddar Stuffed Potatoes

Ingredients:

- 4 large russet potatoes
- 2 cups broccoli florets, chopped
- 1 tablespoon olive oil
- 1 small onion, finely chopped
- 2 cloves garlic, minced
- 1 cup shredded cheddar cheese
- 1/2 cup sour cream or Greek yogurt
- Salt and pepper to taste
- Chopped fresh chives or green onions for garnish (optional)

Instructions:

1. Preheat your oven to 400°F (200°C).
2. Scrub the russet potatoes clean and pierce them several times with a fork.
3. Place the potatoes directly on the oven rack and bake for 45-60 minutes, or until tender when pierced with a fork.
4. While the potatoes are baking, steam the chopped broccoli florets until tender, about 5-7 minutes. Set aside.
5. In a skillet, heat the olive oil over medium heat. Add the finely chopped onion and cook for 3-4 minutes until softened.
6. Add the minced garlic to the skillet and cook for another minute until fragrant.
7. Remove the skillet from heat and set aside.
8. Once the potatoes are baked, remove them from the oven and let them cool slightly.
9. Slice off the top third of each potato lengthwise. Carefully scoop out the flesh from the potatoes, leaving a thin shell intact.
10. In a mixing bowl, combine the scooped-out potato flesh with the cooked onion and garlic mixture, steamed broccoli florets, shredded cheddar cheese, and sour cream or Greek yogurt. Season with salt and pepper to taste.
11. Spoon the broccoli and cheddar filling back into the hollowed-out potato shells.
12. Place the stuffed potatoes on a baking sheet lined with parchment paper.
13. Bake the stuffed potatoes in the preheated oven for an additional 10-15 minutes, or until the filling is heated through and the cheese is melted and bubbly.

14. Remove the stuffed potatoes from the oven and garnish with chopped fresh chives or green onions, if desired.
15. Serve the Broccoli and Cheddar Stuffed Potatoes hot as a delicious and satisfying meal.

These Broccoli and Cheddar Stuffed Potatoes are hearty, flavorful, and perfect for a comforting dinner. Enjoy the creamy filling packed with broccoli and cheddar cheese nestled inside tender baked potatoes!

Green Bean Almondine

Ingredients:

- 1 pound green beans, trimmed
- 2 tablespoons unsalted butter
- 1/4 cup sliced almonds
- 2 cloves garlic, minced
- 1 tablespoon fresh lemon juice
- Salt and pepper to taste
- Fresh parsley, chopped, for garnish (optional)
- Lemon wedges, for serving (optional)

Instructions:

1. Bring a large pot of salted water to a boil. Add the trimmed green beans and blanch them for 2-3 minutes, or until they are bright green and crisp-tender. Drain the beans and immediately plunge them into a bowl of ice water to stop the cooking process. Drain again and set aside.
2. In a large skillet, melt the unsalted butter over medium heat. Add the sliced almonds to the skillet and cook, stirring constantly, for 2-3 minutes, or until the almonds are lightly golden brown and fragrant.
3. Add the minced garlic to the skillet and cook for another minute until fragrant.
4. Add the blanched green beans to the skillet and toss to coat them evenly with the butter, almonds, and garlic. Cook for 2-3 minutes, or until the beans are heated through.
5. Drizzle the fresh lemon juice over the green beans and season with salt and pepper to taste. Toss again to combine.
6. Transfer the Green Bean Almondine to a serving dish and garnish with chopped fresh parsley, if desired.
7. Serve hot, with lemon wedges on the side for squeezing over the beans if desired.

This Green Bean Almondine is a classic side dish that pairs well with a variety of main courses. Enjoy the crisp-tender green beans coated in buttery almonds and garlic, with a hint of fresh lemon juice for brightness!

Arugula and Strawberry Salad with Balsamic Vinaigrette

Ingredients:

For the salad:

- 4 cups fresh arugula
- 1 cup fresh strawberries, hulled and sliced
- 1/4 cup sliced almonds, toasted
- 1/4 cup crumbled feta cheese (optional)
- 1/4 cup thinly sliced red onion (optional)

For the balsamic vinaigrette:

- 3 tablespoons balsamic vinegar
- 1 tablespoon honey or maple syrup
- 1 teaspoon Dijon mustard
- 1/4 cup extra virgin olive oil
- Salt and pepper to taste

Instructions:

1. In a large salad bowl, combine the fresh arugula, sliced strawberries, toasted sliced almonds, crumbled feta cheese (if using), and thinly sliced red onion (if using). Toss gently to combine.
2. In a small bowl or jar, whisk together the balsamic vinegar, honey or maple syrup, and Dijon mustard until well combined.
3. Slowly drizzle in the extra virgin olive oil while whisking continuously until the vinaigrette is emulsified. Season with salt and pepper to taste.
4. Pour the balsamic vinaigrette over the salad and toss gently to coat the ingredients evenly with the dressing.
5. Taste and adjust the seasoning if needed.
6. Serve the Arugula and Strawberry Salad immediately as a refreshing appetizer or side dish.

This Arugula and Strawberry Salad with Balsamic Vinaigrette is a perfect combination of peppery arugula, sweet strawberries, crunchy almonds, and tangy feta cheese, all brought together with a flavorful balsamic vinaigrette. Enjoy the vibrant flavors and textures of this delicious salad!

Summer Vegetable Ratatouille

Ingredients:

- 1 eggplant, diced
- 2 zucchini, diced
- 1 yellow squash, diced
- 1 red bell pepper, diced
- 1 yellow bell pepper, diced
- 1 onion, diced
- 3 cloves garlic, minced
- 4 tomatoes, diced
- 2 tablespoons tomato paste
- 2 tablespoons olive oil
- 2 teaspoons dried thyme
- 2 teaspoons dried oregano
- Salt and pepper to taste
- Fresh basil leaves for garnish (optional)

Instructions:

1. Heat the olive oil in a large skillet or Dutch oven over medium heat.
2. Add the diced onion and cook until softened, about 5 minutes.
3. Add the minced garlic to the skillet and cook for another minute until fragrant.
4. Add the diced eggplant, zucchini, yellow squash, red bell pepper, and yellow bell pepper to the skillet. Cook, stirring occasionally, for about 10 minutes, or until the vegetables start to soften.
5. Stir in the diced tomatoes, tomato paste, dried thyme, dried oregano, salt, and pepper.
6. Reduce the heat to low, cover the skillet, and let the ratatouille simmer for 20-25 minutes, stirring occasionally, until the vegetables are tender and the flavors have melded together.
7. Taste and adjust the seasoning with salt and pepper if needed.
8. Once cooked, remove the ratatouille from heat and let it cool slightly.
9. Serve the Summer Vegetable Ratatouille warm, garnished with fresh basil leaves if desired.

This Summer Vegetable Ratatouille is a colorful and flavorful dish that celebrates the bounty of summer produce. Enjoy the tender vegetables and aromatic herbs in every bite!

Potato Leek Soup

Ingredients:

- 3 large leeks, white and light green parts only, cleaned and thinly sliced
- 3 tablespoons unsalted butter or olive oil
- 3 cloves garlic, minced
- 4 cups potatoes, peeled and diced
- 6 cups vegetable or chicken broth
- 1 bay leaf
- 1 teaspoon dried thyme
- Salt and pepper to taste
- 1 cup heavy cream or half-and-half (optional)
- Chopped fresh chives or parsley for garnish (optional)

Instructions:

1. In a large pot or Dutch oven, melt the butter or heat the olive oil over medium heat.
2. Add the sliced leeks to the pot and sauté for 5-7 minutes, stirring occasionally, until they are softened and translucent.
3. Add the minced garlic to the pot and cook for another minute until fragrant.
4. Add the diced potatoes, vegetable or chicken broth, bay leaf, dried thyme, salt, and pepper to the pot. Stir to combine.
5. Bring the soup to a boil, then reduce the heat to low and let it simmer, partially covered, for about 20-25 minutes, or until the potatoes are tender.
6. Once the potatoes are cooked, remove the bay leaf from the soup.
7. Using an immersion blender, blend the soup until smooth and creamy. Alternatively, you can transfer the soup in batches to a blender and blend until smooth, then return it to the pot.
8. If using, stir in the heavy cream or half-and-half to the soup until well combined. Adjust the seasoning with salt and pepper to taste.
9. Heat the soup over low heat until warmed through, but do not boil.
10. Ladle the Potato Leek Soup into bowls and garnish with chopped fresh chives or parsley, if desired.
11. Serve the soup hot with crusty bread or your favorite accompaniment.

This Potato Leek Soup is creamy, flavorful, and perfect for a cozy meal. Enjoy the comforting combination of tender potatoes, aromatic leeks, and savory herbs in every spoonful!

Stuffed Acorn Squash with Wild Rice and Cranberries

Ingredients:

- 2 acorn squash, halved and seeds removed
- 1 cup wild rice, rinsed
- 2 cups vegetable broth or water
- 1 tablespoon olive oil
- 1 small onion, finely chopped
- 2 cloves garlic, minced
- 1 stalk celery, finely chopped
- 1/2 cup dried cranberries
- 1/4 cup chopped pecans or walnuts (optional)
- 2 tablespoons chopped fresh parsley
- 1 teaspoon dried thyme
- Salt and pepper to taste
- Grated Parmesan cheese for serving (optional)

Instructions:

1. Preheat your oven to 375°F (190°C).
2. Place the acorn squash halves cut side down on a baking sheet lined with parchment paper. Bake in the preheated oven for 30-35 minutes, or until the squash is tender when pierced with a fork.
3. While the squash is baking, prepare the wild rice. In a medium saucepan, combine the rinsed wild rice and vegetable broth or water. Bring to a boil, then reduce the heat to low, cover, and simmer for 40-45 minutes, or until the rice is tender and the liquid is absorbed. Remove from heat and set aside.
4. In a large skillet, heat the olive oil over medium heat. Add the chopped onion and celery to the skillet and cook for 5-7 minutes, or until softened.
5. Add the minced garlic to the skillet and cook for another minute until fragrant.
6. Stir in the cooked wild rice, dried cranberries, chopped pecans or walnuts (if using), chopped fresh parsley, dried thyme, salt, and pepper. Cook for an additional 2-3 minutes to heat through and allow the flavors to meld together.
7. Once the squash halves are baked and tender, remove them from the oven. Flip them over so the cut side is facing up.
8. Fill each acorn squash half with the wild rice stuffing mixture, packing it down slightly.

9. Return the stuffed acorn squash halves to the oven and bake for an additional 10-15 minutes, or until heated through.
10. Once baked, remove the stuffed acorn squash from the oven and let them cool slightly before serving.
11. Optionally, sprinkle grated Parmesan cheese over the top of each stuffed squash half before serving.

This Stuffed Acorn Squash with Wild Rice and Cranberries is a flavorful and satisfying dish that's perfect for a cozy dinner. Enjoy the combination of tender roasted squash, hearty wild rice, and sweet cranberries in every bite!

Roasted Brussels Sprouts with Bacon and Maple Syrup

Ingredients:

- 1 pound Brussels sprouts, trimmed and halved
- 4 slices bacon, chopped
- 2 tablespoons maple syrup
- 2 tablespoons olive oil
- Salt and pepper to taste

Instructions:

1. Preheat your oven to 400°F (200°C).
2. In a large mixing bowl, toss the halved Brussels sprouts with olive oil, salt, and pepper until evenly coated.
3. Spread the Brussels sprouts in a single layer on a baking sheet lined with parchment paper.
4. Roast the Brussels sprouts in the preheated oven for 20-25 minutes, or until they are golden brown and tender, stirring halfway through the cooking time for even roasting.
5. While the Brussels sprouts are roasting, cook the chopped bacon in a skillet over medium heat until crispy. Remove the cooked bacon from the skillet and place it on a plate lined with paper towels to drain excess grease.
6. Once the Brussels sprouts are roasted, remove them from the oven and transfer them to a serving dish.
7. Drizzle the roasted Brussels sprouts with maple syrup and sprinkle the crispy bacon over the top.
8. Toss the Brussels sprouts, bacon, and maple syrup together until evenly combined.
9. Serve the Roasted Brussels Sprouts with Bacon and Maple Syrup hot as a delicious side dish.

This Roasted Brussels Sprouts with Bacon and Maple Syrup dish is a delightful combination of savory and sweet flavors, with crispy bacon adding a delicious crunch to the tender Brussels sprouts. Enjoy this flavorful and comforting side dish!

Grilled Peaches with Honey and Yogurt

Ingredients:

- 4 ripe peaches, halved and pitted
- 2 tablespoons honey
- 1 cup Greek yogurt
- Fresh mint leaves for garnish (optional)

Instructions:

1. Preheat your grill to medium-high heat.
2. Brush the cut sides of the peach halves with a little honey.
3. Place the peach halves cut side down on the preheated grill.
4. Grill the peaches for 3-4 minutes, or until they develop grill marks and caramelize slightly.
5. Carefully flip the peach halves using tongs and grill for an additional 2-3 minutes on the other side.
6. Once the peaches are grilled to your liking and softened, remove them from the grill and let them cool slightly.
7. To serve, place a grilled peach half on each plate. Top each peach half with a dollop of Greek yogurt and drizzle with additional honey.
8. Garnish with fresh mint leaves if desired.
9. Serve the Grilled Peaches with Honey and Yogurt immediately as a delicious and refreshing dessert.

These Grilled Peaches with Honey and Yogurt are a delightful summer treat, showcasing the natural sweetness of ripe peaches complemented by the creamy Greek yogurt and floral honey. Enjoy the contrast of warm grilled fruit with cool yogurt for a simple yet elegant dessert!

Eggplant Parmesan

Ingredients:

- 2 medium-sized eggplants, sliced into 1/4-inch rounds
- Salt
- 2 cups breadcrumbs (you can use Italian-seasoned breadcrumbs or plain breadcrumbs mixed with Italian seasoning)
- 1 cup all-purpose flour
- 3 large eggs, beaten
- Vegetable oil, for frying
- 2 cups marinara sauce
- 2 cups shredded mozzarella cheese
- 1/2 cup grated Parmesan cheese
- Fresh basil leaves for garnish (optional)

Instructions:

1. Place the eggplant slices in a colander and sprinkle them with salt. Let them sit for about 30 minutes to draw out excess moisture. After 30 minutes, rinse the eggplant slices under cold water and pat them dry with paper towels.
2. Preheat your oven to 375°F (190°C).
3. Set up a breading station with three shallow dishes: one with flour, one with beaten eggs, and one with breadcrumbs.
4. Dredge each eggplant slice in the flour, shaking off any excess. Dip it into the beaten eggs, allowing any excess to drip off. Then coat it in the breadcrumbs, pressing gently to adhere. Repeat with the remaining eggplant slices.
5. Heat vegetable oil in a large skillet over medium-high heat. Working in batches, fry the breaded eggplant slices for about 2-3 minutes on each side, or until golden brown and crispy. Transfer the fried eggplant slices to a paper towel-lined plate to drain any excess oil.
6. Spread a thin layer of marinara sauce on the bottom of a 9x13-inch baking dish. Place a layer of fried eggplant slices on top of the sauce. Sprinkle some shredded mozzarella and grated Parmesan cheese over the eggplant slices. Repeat the layers, finishing with a layer of marinara sauce and a generous sprinkle of cheese on top.

7. Cover the baking dish with aluminum foil and bake in the preheated oven for 25 minutes.
8. After 25 minutes, remove the foil and continue baking for an additional 10-15 minutes, or until the cheese is melted and bubbly and the eggplant is tender.
9. Once baked, let the Eggplant Parmesan rest for a few minutes before serving. Garnish with fresh basil leaves, if desired.
10. Serve the Eggplant Parmesan hot as a delicious and comforting meal.

This Eggplant Parmesan is a classic Italian dish that features tender eggplant slices coated in crispy breadcrumbs, layered with marinara sauce, and topped with melted mozzarella and Parmesan cheese. Enjoy the rich and comforting flavors of this timeless dish!

Roasted Root Vegetable Medley

Ingredients:

- 2 large carrots, peeled and cut into chunks
- 2 parsnips, peeled and cut into chunks
- 2 beets, peeled and cut into chunks
- 2 sweet potatoes, peeled and cut into chunks
- 1 red onion, peeled and cut into wedges
- 4 cloves garlic, minced
- 3 tablespoons olive oil
- 1 teaspoon dried thyme
- 1 teaspoon dried rosemary
- Salt and pepper to taste
- Fresh parsley for garnish (optional)

Instructions:

1. Preheat your oven to 400°F (200°C).
2. In a large mixing bowl, combine the carrot chunks, parsnip chunks, beet chunks, sweet potato chunks, onion wedges, and minced garlic.
3. Drizzle olive oil over the vegetables and toss to coat them evenly.
4. Sprinkle dried thyme, dried rosemary, salt, and pepper over the vegetables and toss again to distribute the seasonings.
5. Spread the seasoned vegetables in a single layer on a baking sheet lined with parchment paper or aluminum foil.
6. Roast the vegetables in the preheated oven for 30-35 minutes, or until they are tender and caramelized, stirring halfway through the cooking time for even roasting.
7. Once the vegetables are roasted to your liking, remove them from the oven and transfer them to a serving dish.
8. Garnish the Roasted Root Vegetable Medley with fresh parsley, if desired, before serving.
9. Serve the roasted vegetables hot as a flavorful and nutritious side dish.

This Roasted Root Vegetable Medley is a colorful and delicious dish that showcases the natural sweetness and earthy flavors of seasonal root vegetables. Enjoy the tender and caramelized vegetables as a satisfying accompaniment to any meal!

Tomato and Basil Frittata

Ingredients:

- 8 large eggs
- 1/4 cup milk or heavy cream
- 1 tablespoon olive oil
- 1 small onion, diced
- 2 cloves garlic, minced
- 1 cup cherry tomatoes, halved
- 1/4 cup fresh basil leaves, chopped
- Salt and pepper to taste
- 1/2 cup shredded mozzarella cheese (optional)
- Grated Parmesan cheese for serving (optional)
- Fresh basil leaves for garnish (optional)

Instructions:

1. Preheat your oven to 350°F (175°C).
2. In a large mixing bowl, whisk together the eggs and milk or heavy cream until well combined. Season with salt and pepper to taste. Set aside.
3. Heat the olive oil in an oven-safe skillet (preferably non-stick) over medium heat.
4. Add the diced onion to the skillet and sauté for 3-4 minutes, or until softened and translucent.
5. Add the minced garlic to the skillet and cook for another minute until fragrant.
6. Add the halved cherry tomatoes to the skillet and cook for 2-3 minutes, or until they start to soften.
7. Sprinkle the chopped fresh basil leaves over the tomato mixture in the skillet.
8. Pour the egg mixture evenly over the tomato and basil mixture in the skillet. Stir gently to distribute the ingredients.
9. Cook the frittata on the stovetop for 3-4 minutes, or until the edges begin to set.
10. If using shredded mozzarella cheese, sprinkle it evenly over the top of the frittata.
11. Transfer the skillet to the preheated oven and bake the frittata for 10-15 minutes, or until the eggs are set and the top is lightly golden brown.
12. Once cooked, remove the frittata from the oven and let it cool slightly.
13. Slice the Tomato and Basil Frittata into wedges and serve warm, garnished with grated Parmesan cheese and fresh basil leaves if desired.

This Tomato and Basil Frittata is a flavorful and versatile dish that can be enjoyed for breakfast, brunch, lunch, or dinner. The combination of juicy cherry tomatoes, aromatic basil, and creamy eggs makes for a delicious and satisfying meal!

Cabbage and Apple Slaw

Ingredients:

- 4 cups shredded cabbage (green or red cabbage, or a combination)
- 2 medium apples, cored and thinly sliced (choose a sweet variety like Fuji or Gala)
- 1/2 cup thinly sliced red onion
- 1/4 cup chopped fresh parsley or cilantro
- 1/4 cup chopped toasted walnuts or pecans (optional, for added crunch)
- 1/4 cup mayonnaise
- 2 tablespoons apple cider vinegar
- 1 tablespoon honey or maple syrup
- 1 teaspoon Dijon mustard
- Salt and pepper to taste

Instructions:

1. In a large mixing bowl, combine the shredded cabbage, sliced apples, sliced red onion, chopped fresh parsley or cilantro, and chopped toasted walnuts or pecans (if using).
2. In a small bowl, whisk together the mayonnaise, apple cider vinegar, honey or maple syrup, Dijon mustard, salt, and pepper until well combined.
3. Pour the dressing over the cabbage and apple mixture in the large mixing bowl.
4. Toss the ingredients together until the cabbage and apples are evenly coated with the dressing.
5. Taste and adjust the seasoning with salt and pepper if needed.
6. Cover the bowl with plastic wrap and refrigerate the slaw for at least 30 minutes to allow the flavors to meld together.
7. Before serving, give the slaw a final toss to redistribute the dressing.
8. Serve the Cabbage and Apple Slaw chilled as a refreshing side dish or topping for sandwiches, tacos, or grilled meats.

This Cabbage and Apple Slaw is a delicious combination of crunchy cabbage, sweet and tangy apples, and flavorful dressing. Enjoy its refreshing taste and vibrant colors as a perfect complement to a variety of dishes!

Grilled Halloumi with Watermelon and Mint

Ingredients:

- 1 block of halloumi cheese, sliced into 1/2-inch thick pieces
- 2 cups cubed watermelon
- Fresh mint leaves
- Olive oil, for brushing
- Balsamic glaze or reduction, for drizzling (optional)
- Salt and pepper to taste

Instructions:

1. Preheat your grill or grill pan over medium-high heat.
2. Brush both sides of the halloumi slices with olive oil to prevent sticking.
3. Place the halloumi slices on the grill and cook for 2-3 minutes on each side, or until grill marks appear and the cheese is warmed through.
4. While the halloumi is grilling, prepare the watermelon by cubing it into bite-sized pieces.
5. Arrange the grilled halloumi slices and cubed watermelon on a serving platter.
6. Sprinkle fresh mint leaves over the top of the halloumi and watermelon.
7. Season with salt and pepper to taste.
8. If desired, drizzle balsamic glaze or reduction over the grilled halloumi and watermelon for added flavor.
9. Serve the Grilled Halloumi with Watermelon and Mint immediately as a refreshing appetizer or light summer snack.

This Grilled Halloumi with Watermelon and Mint dish is a delightful combination of savory, sweet, and refreshing flavors. Enjoy the contrast of the warm, salty halloumi with the cool, juicy watermelon, complemented by the aromatic freshness of mint!

Garlic Butter Roasted Mushrooms

Ingredients:

- 1 pound mushrooms (such as cremini or button mushrooms), cleaned and halved or quartered if large
- 3 tablespoons unsalted butter, melted
- 3 cloves garlic, minced
- 2 tablespoons chopped fresh parsley
- Salt and pepper to taste

Instructions:

1. Preheat your oven to 400°F (200°C).
2. In a large mixing bowl, combine the cleaned and halved mushrooms with melted butter, minced garlic, chopped fresh parsley, salt, and pepper. Toss until the mushrooms are evenly coated with the butter and seasoning.
3. Spread the coated mushrooms in a single layer on a baking sheet lined with parchment paper.
4. Roast the mushrooms in the preheated oven for 20-25 minutes, or until they are golden brown and tender, stirring halfway through the cooking time for even roasting.
5. Once roasted to your liking, remove the mushrooms from the oven and transfer them to a serving dish.
6. Serve the Garlic Butter Roasted Mushrooms hot as a delicious and flavorful side dish or appetizer.

These Garlic Butter Roasted Mushrooms are bursting with flavor and aroma, making them a perfect accompaniment to any meal. Enjoy the rich, savory taste of roasted mushrooms combined with the fragrant garlic butter and fresh parsley!

Kale Caesar Salad with Homemade Dressing

Ingredients:

For the salad:

- 1 large bunch kale, stems removed and leaves torn into bite-sized pieces
- 1 cup croutons (store-bought or homemade)
- 1/4 cup grated Parmesan cheese
- Lemon wedges for serving (optional)

For the dressing:

- 1/2 cup mayonnaise
- 2 tablespoons grated Parmesan cheese
- 2 tablespoons freshly squeezed lemon juice
- 1 tablespoon Dijon mustard
- 1 clove garlic, minced
- 1 teaspoon Worcestershire sauce
- Salt and pepper to taste
- 2 tablespoons extra virgin olive oil

Instructions:

1. In a large mixing bowl, add the torn kale leaves.
2. In a separate small bowl, whisk together the mayonnaise, grated Parmesan cheese, lemon juice, Dijon mustard, minced garlic, Worcestershire sauce, salt, and pepper until smooth and well combined.
3. Slowly drizzle in the olive oil while whisking continuously until the dressing is emulsified.
4. Pour the dressing over the kale leaves in the large mixing bowl. Toss until the kale leaves are evenly coated with the dressing.
5. Let the kale salad sit for about 10-15 minutes to allow the dressing to soften the kale leaves slightly.
6. Before serving, add the croutons and grated Parmesan cheese to the kale salad. Toss to combine.
7. Taste and adjust the seasoning with salt and pepper if needed.

8. Serve the Kale Caesar Salad with Lemon wedges on the side for squeezing over the salad if desired.

This Kale Caesar Salad with Homemade Dressing is a nutritious and flavorful twist on the classic Caesar salad. Enjoy the hearty texture of kale paired with the creamy homemade dressing and crunchy croutons for a satisfying and delicious salad experience!

Baked Parmesan Zucchini Fries

Ingredients:

- 2 medium zucchini, cut into fry-shaped sticks
- 1/2 cup grated Parmesan cheese
- 1/2 cup breadcrumbs (you can use regular breadcrumbs or panko breadcrumbs for extra crunch)
- 1 teaspoon garlic powder
- 1 teaspoon dried oregano
- 1/2 teaspoon paprika
- Salt and pepper to taste
- 2 large eggs, beaten
- Cooking spray or olive oil for greasing

Instructions:

1. Preheat your oven to 425°F (220°C). Line a baking sheet with parchment paper or aluminum foil and lightly grease it with cooking spray or olive oil.
2. In a shallow dish, combine the grated Parmesan cheese, breadcrumbs, garlic powder, dried oregano, paprika, salt, and pepper. Mix well to combine.
3. Place the beaten eggs in another shallow dish.
4. Dip each zucchini stick into the beaten eggs, shaking off any excess.
5. Roll the egg-coated zucchini stick in the Parmesan breadcrumb mixture, pressing gently to adhere the coating.
6. Place the coated zucchini stick on the prepared baking sheet in a single layer, leaving space between each stick.
7. Repeat the process with the remaining zucchini sticks.
8. Lightly spray the coated zucchini sticks with cooking spray or drizzle with olive oil.
9. Bake in the preheated oven for 20-25 minutes, or until the zucchini fries are golden brown and crispy, flipping halfway through the cooking time for even browning.
10. Once baked, remove the zucchini fries from the oven and let them cool slightly before serving.
11. Serve the Baked Parmesan Zucchini Fries hot as a delicious and healthier alternative to traditional fries.

These Baked Parmesan Zucchini Fries are crispy on the outside, tender on the inside, and bursting with flavor from the Parmesan cheese and seasonings. Enjoy them as a tasty snack, appetizer, or side dish!

Beetroot and Goat Cheese Tartlets

Ingredients:

For the pastry:

- 1 1/4 cups all-purpose flour
- 1/2 teaspoon salt
- 1/2 cup cold unsalted butter, cut into small cubes
- 2-3 tablespoons ice water

For the filling:

- 2 medium-sized beetroots, cooked, peeled, and thinly sliced
- 4 ounces goat cheese, crumbled
- 2 tablespoons honey
- 1 tablespoon balsamic vinegar
- Fresh thyme leaves for garnish (optional)
- Salt and pepper to taste

Instructions:

1. Preheat your oven to 375°F (190°C).
2. In a food processor, combine the all-purpose flour and salt. Add the cold cubed butter and pulse until the mixture resembles coarse crumbs.
3. With the food processor running, gradually add the ice water, 1 tablespoon at a time, until the dough comes together and forms a ball.
4. Turn the dough out onto a lightly floured surface and shape it into a disk. Wrap the dough in plastic wrap and refrigerate for at least 30 minutes.
5. Once chilled, roll out the dough on a lightly floured surface to about 1/8 inch thickness. Cut out circles slightly larger than the wells of your tartlet pan.
6. Press the dough circles into the wells of the tartlet pan, trimming any excess dough from the edges. Prick the bottom of the tartlet shells with a fork.
7. Line the tartlet shells with parchment paper and fill them with pie weights or dried beans.

8. Blind bake the tartlet shells in the preheated oven for 10-12 minutes, or until the edges are lightly golden brown.
9. Remove the parchment paper and pie weights from the tartlet shells and let them cool slightly.
10. While the tartlet shells are cooling, prepare the filling. In a small bowl, whisk together the honey and balsamic vinegar.
11. Arrange the thinly sliced beetroot in the tartlet shells. Drizzle the honey and balsamic mixture over the beetroot slices.
12. Sprinkle crumbled goat cheese over the top of each tartlet.
13. Season with salt and pepper to taste.
14. Bake the tartlets in the preheated oven for an additional 10-12 minutes, or until the cheese is melted and bubbly.
15. Once baked, remove the tartlets from the oven and let them cool slightly before serving.
16. Garnish the Beetroot and Goat Cheese Tartlets with fresh thyme leaves, if desired, before serving.

These Beetroot and Goat Cheese Tartlets are a delightful combination of earthy beetroots, tangy goat cheese, and sweet honey, all nestled in a flaky pastry shell. Enjoy them as an elegant appetizer or light meal!

Corn and Tomato Pie

Ingredients:

For the crust:

- 1 1/4 cups all-purpose flour
- 1/2 teaspoon salt
- 1/2 cup unsalted butter, chilled and cut into small pieces
- 3-4 tablespoons ice water

For the filling:

- 3 cups fresh corn kernels (about 4 ears of corn)
- 1 cup cherry tomatoes, halved
- 1/2 cup grated sharp cheddar cheese
- 1/4 cup grated Parmesan cheese
- 1/4 cup mayonnaise
- 1/4 cup sour cream or Greek yogurt
- 2 cloves garlic, minced
- 1 tablespoon fresh basil, chopped
- 1 tablespoon fresh chives, chopped
- Salt and pepper to taste

Instructions:

1. Preheat your oven to 375°F (190°C).
2. To make the crust, in a food processor, combine the all-purpose flour and salt. Add the chilled butter pieces and pulse until the mixture resembles coarse crumbs.
3. With the food processor running, gradually add the ice water, 1 tablespoon at a time, until the dough comes together and forms a ball.
4. Turn the dough out onto a lightly floured surface and shape it into a disk. Wrap the dough in plastic wrap and refrigerate for at least 30 minutes.

5. Once chilled, roll out the dough on a lightly floured surface to fit a 9-inch pie dish. Press the dough into the pie dish and trim any excess dough from the edges. Crimp the edges of the crust with a fork or your fingers.
6. In a large mixing bowl, combine the fresh corn kernels, halved cherry tomatoes, grated cheddar cheese, grated Parmesan cheese, mayonnaise, sour cream or Greek yogurt, minced garlic, chopped basil, chopped chives, salt, and pepper. Stir until well combined.
7. Pour the corn and tomato mixture into the prepared pie crust, spreading it out evenly.
8. Bake the pie in the preheated oven for 30-35 minutes, or until the filling is set and the crust is golden brown.
9. Once baked, remove the pie from the oven and let it cool slightly before slicing.
10. Serve the Corn and Tomato Pie warm or at room temperature as a delicious and flavorful summer dish.

This Corn and Tomato Pie is a delightful combination of sweet corn, juicy tomatoes, and savory cheese, all nestled in a flaky, buttery crust. Enjoy it as a main dish or a side dish for brunch, lunch, or dinner!

Butternut Squash and Sage Risotto

Ingredients:

- 1 small butternut squash, peeled, seeded, and diced into small cubes
- 6 cups vegetable or chicken broth
- 2 tablespoons olive oil
- 1 small onion, finely chopped
- 2 cloves garlic, minced
- 1 1/2 cups Arborio rice
- 1/2 cup dry white wine (optional)
- 1/4 cup grated Parmesan cheese
- 2 tablespoons unsalted butter
- 1 tablespoon chopped fresh sage leaves
- Salt and pepper to taste
- Additional grated Parmesan cheese and sage leaves for garnish (optional)

Instructions:

1. In a saucepan, bring the vegetable or chicken broth to a simmer. Keep it warm over low heat.
2. In a large skillet or Dutch oven, heat the olive oil over medium heat. Add the diced butternut squash and cook, stirring occasionally, for about 8-10 minutes, or until the squash is tender and lightly caramelized. Remove the squash from the skillet and set aside.
3. In the same skillet, add a bit more olive oil if needed. Add the chopped onion and cook for 3-4 minutes, or until softened.
4. Add the minced garlic to the skillet and cook for another minute until fragrant.
5. Stir in the Arborio rice and cook for 1-2 minutes, stirring constantly, until the rice is lightly toasted.
6. If using, pour in the dry white wine and cook, stirring occasionally, until the wine is absorbed by the rice.
7. Begin adding the warm broth to the skillet, one ladleful at a time, stirring frequently. Wait until each ladle of broth is absorbed before adding more.
8. Continue adding the broth and stirring the rice for about 18-20 minutes, or until the rice is creamy and tender, but still slightly al dente.

9. Stir in the cooked butternut squash, grated Parmesan cheese, unsalted butter, and chopped fresh sage leaves. Season with salt and pepper to taste.
10. Cook for an additional 2-3 minutes, or until the butternut squash is heated through and the risotto has reached your desired consistency.
11. Remove the risotto from the heat and let it rest for a few minutes.
12. Serve the Butternut Squash and Sage Risotto hot, garnished with additional grated Parmesan cheese and sage leaves if desired.

This Butternut Squash and Sage Risotto is creamy, comforting, and bursting with autumn flavors. Enjoy it as a delicious main dish or as a side dish alongside roasted meats or poultry.

Swiss Chard and Ricotta Stuffed Shells

Ingredients:

For the stuffed shells:

- 20 jumbo pasta shells
- 1 bunch Swiss chard, stems removed and leaves chopped
- 15 ounces ricotta cheese
- 1 cup shredded mozzarella cheese
- 1/2 cup grated Parmesan cheese
- 2 cloves garlic, minced
- 1 tablespoon olive oil
- Salt and pepper to taste

For the tomato sauce:

- 24 ounces marinara sauce
- 2 tablespoons tomato paste
- 1 teaspoon dried Italian herbs (such as oregano, basil, and thyme)
- Salt and pepper to taste

Instructions:

1. Preheat your oven to 375°F (190°C). Lightly grease a 9x13-inch baking dish with olive oil or cooking spray.
2. Cook the jumbo pasta shells according to the package instructions until al dente. Drain and set aside.
3. In a large skillet, heat the olive oil over medium heat. Add the minced garlic and chopped Swiss chard leaves to the skillet. Cook, stirring occasionally, for about 5-6 minutes, or until the Swiss chard is wilted and tender. Remove from heat and let it cool slightly.
4. In a mixing bowl, combine the ricotta cheese, shredded mozzarella cheese, grated Parmesan cheese, cooked Swiss chard, salt, and pepper. Stir until well combined.

5. In another bowl, mix together the marinara sauce, tomato paste, dried Italian herbs, salt, and pepper to make the tomato sauce.
6. Spoon a thin layer of the tomato sauce into the bottom of the prepared baking dish.
7. Stuff each cooked jumbo pasta shell with a generous amount of the Swiss chard and ricotta mixture. Place the stuffed shells in the baking dish in a single layer.
8. Pour the remaining tomato sauce over the stuffed shells, covering them evenly.
9. Cover the baking dish with aluminum foil and bake in the preheated oven for 25-30 minutes, or until the sauce is bubbly and the shells are heated through.
10. Remove the foil and sprinkle additional grated Parmesan cheese over the top, if desired.
11. Return the baking dish to the oven and bake, uncovered, for an additional 5-10 minutes, or until the cheese is melted and lightly golden brown.
12. Once baked, remove the Swiss Chard and Ricotta Stuffed Shells from the oven and let them cool for a few minutes before serving.

This Swiss Chard and Ricotta Stuffed Shells dish is a comforting and flavorful meal that's perfect for a family dinner or special occasion. Enjoy the combination of creamy ricotta cheese, hearty Swiss chard, and savory tomato sauce in every bite!

Grilled Vegetable Quesadillas

Ingredients:

For the grilled vegetables:

- 1 red bell pepper, sliced into strips
- 1 yellow bell pepper, sliced into strips
- 1 zucchini, sliced into rounds
- 1 yellow squash, sliced into rounds
- 1 red onion, sliced into rounds
- 2 tablespoons olive oil
- Salt and pepper to taste
- 1 teaspoon chili powder (optional)
- 1 teaspoon ground cumin (optional)
- 1 teaspoon paprika (optional)

For the quesadillas:

- 8 large flour tortillas
- 2 cups shredded cheese (such as cheddar, Monterey Jack, or a Mexican cheese blend)
- 1/2 cup chopped fresh cilantro (optional)
- Salsa, guacamole, and sour cream for serving

Instructions:

1. Preheat your grill to medium-high heat.
2. In a large bowl, toss the sliced bell peppers, zucchini, yellow squash, and red onion with olive oil, salt, pepper, and any optional spices like chili powder, cumin, and paprika.
3. Place the seasoned vegetables on the grill and cook for about 5-7 minutes per side, or until they are tender and slightly charred. Remove from the grill and set aside.

4. To assemble the quesadillas, lay out four tortillas on a flat surface. Sprinkle each tortilla with a portion of shredded cheese.
5. Top the cheese with a generous portion of grilled vegetables, spreading them out evenly.
6. Sprinkle chopped cilantro over the vegetables, if using.
7. Place another tortilla on top of each assembled quesadilla to form a sandwich.
8. Heat a large skillet or grill pan over medium heat. Place one quesadilla in the skillet and cook for 2-3 minutes per side, or until the tortillas are golden brown and the cheese is melted.
9. Repeat with the remaining quesadillas.
10. Once cooked, remove the quesadillas from the skillet and let them cool for a minute before slicing into wedges.
11. Serve the Grilled Vegetable Quesadillas hot with salsa, guacamole, and sour cream on the side for dipping.

These Grilled Vegetable Quesadillas are loaded with flavorful grilled vegetables and gooey melted cheese, all sandwiched between crispy tortillas. They make for a delicious and satisfying meal or appetizer that's perfect for a summer cookout or weeknight dinner!

Roasted Pumpkin Soup with Crispy Sage

Ingredients:

- 1 small pumpkin (about 3-4 pounds), peeled, seeded, and cut into chunks
- 2 tablespoons olive oil
- 1 onion, chopped
- 2 cloves garlic, minced
- 4 cups vegetable or chicken broth
- 1 cup coconut milk or heavy cream
- Salt and pepper to taste
- Fresh sage leaves
- 2 tablespoons butter

Instructions:

1. Preheat your oven to 400°F (200°C).
2. Place the pumpkin chunks on a baking sheet. Drizzle with olive oil and season with salt and pepper. Toss to coat evenly.
3. Roast the pumpkin in the preheated oven for 25-30 minutes, or until tender and caramelized.
4. In a large pot or Dutch oven, heat some olive oil over medium heat. Add the chopped onion and cook until softened, about 5 minutes.
5. Add the minced garlic to the pot and cook for another minute until fragrant.
6. Add the roasted pumpkin chunks to the pot and pour in the vegetable or chicken broth. Bring to a simmer and let it cook for 10-15 minutes, allowing the flavors to meld together.

7. Use an immersion blender to puree the soup until smooth. Alternatively, you can transfer the soup to a blender and blend in batches until smooth. Be careful when blending hot liquids.
8. Stir in the coconut milk or heavy cream, and season with additional salt and pepper to taste.
9. In a small skillet, melt the butter over medium heat. Add the fresh sage leaves to the skillet and cook for 1-2 minutes on each side, or until crispy.
10. Ladle the roasted pumpkin soup into bowls and garnish with the crispy sage leaves.
11. Serve the soup hot, optionally with a dollop of sour cream or a drizzle of olive oil on top.

This Roasted Pumpkin Soup with Crispy Sage is creamy, comforting, and bursting with flavor. Enjoy it as a cozy fall or winter meal, perfect for warming up on chilly days!